GOLF'S NEW RULES:

A HANDY FAST REFERENCE

EFFECTIVE 2019

GOLFWELL

Team Golfwell

www.TeamGolfwell.com

Published by: Pacific Trust Holdings NZ Ltd., 2018

HOW THIS BOOKLET WORKS

The USGA and R & A adopted the most major changes to the Rules of Golf in more than 30 years and all go into effect January 1, 2019.

This Booklet, "Golf's New Rules" gives you a clear and quick description of the new rules.

The next page has a quick reference called "Summary of the Changes" which will answer most new rule questions in seconds.

You don't have to remember all the new changes if you keep this booklet in your bag or on your phone for fast answers to new rule questions.

Happy golfing!

Sincerely,

The Team at Golfwell

www.TeamGolfwell.com

SUMMARY OF THE CHANGES

(Made by USGA and the R&A)

Embedded Ball in Rough – You can have a free drop from rough, semi-rough and fairway [1]

Club Length – It's the longest club in bag except putter [2]

Drop from Knee Height – No more dropping from shoulder height [3]

Penalty Areas – Allows for lateral drops and grounding your club, etc. [4]

Substituting a ball – allowed when taking free or penalty relief [5]

Search Time for Lost Ball – Reduced from 5 minutes to 3 minutes [6]

Moving Your Ball While Searching – No penalty if accidental [7]

Lost Ball or Out of Bounds – New option for fairway relief with 2 stroke penalty [8]

Your Ball Accidentally Strikes You, Equipment, etc. – No penalty [9]

Pace of Play – Encourage 40 second time limit to play shot [10]

Ready Golf – Players can agree to play ready golf [11]

Removing Loose Impediments from Bunkers – Allowed now [12]

New Bunker Option – Drop outside the bunker back along the line into the bunker - with 2 shot penalty [13]

Repairing Damage on the Green Without Penalty – You can repair most all damage except normal damage [14]

Line of play on the putting green – You can touch the line [15]

Accidentally Moving Your Ball on the Green No penalty [16]

Hitting the Flagstick No penalty for putt hitting flagstick [17]

Double Hitting the Ball - No penalty, counts as one stroke and play next ball where it lies [18]

Damaged Club - Player can use or repair a damaged club [19]

Replacing Damaged Club – Allowed if damage was caused by "outside influence" or "natural forces" [20]

Distance Measuring Devices – Now allowed unless course prohibits them [21]

Maximum Score – Allows a player to pick up and take maximum score without penalty [22]

Code of Conduct Violations – May result in Disqualification (DQ) [23]

Table of Contents

GOLF'S NEW RULES

Embedded Ball in Rough. Under the old rule, you could only remove and replace an embedded ball if it was embedded in the fairway.

Under the new rule, you can take a free drop if your ball is embedded in the rough or semi-rough as well as the fairway (except when embedded in sand or penalty areas).

If your ball is embedded in the fairway, rough or semi-rough, take a free drop from a point behind the ball and within one club length in the same area where the ball was embedded. (Rule 16.3.)

When your ball is embedded in the sand or a penalty area, the ball must be played as it lies. However, and this may be a gray area, but if a ball is embedded in sand on the fairway, there seems to be free relief allowed if the sand is in an area cut to fairway height or less. This would in effect mean that you can get relief for a ball embedded in a sand filled divot or drain on the fairway provided the sand is in an area cut to fairway height or less and the ball is embedded in its own pitch mark (Rule 16.3a and exceptions).

Club Length. The new rule provides a club length is measured by the longest club in your bag except for your putter (the new rule is designed to avoid measuring a club length with long-shafted putters).

Drop from Knee Height. Under the old rule, you had to hold the ball at shoulder height and drop it.

Under the new rule you must drop the ball from your knee height. (Rule 14.3)

A player might accidentally (or out of old habit) drop from shoulder height. If this happens, there is no penalty and the player must pick up his ball and drop it again from knee height.

When the player drops the ball from knee height, the ball on its way down and before it strikes the ground cannot touch any part of the player's body or equipment. Otherwise the player must drop it again without penalty.

A ball must be dropped in a relief area and come to rest in that relief area. If it rolls out, drop it again and if it rolls out a second time, place the ball where it hit the ground the second time in the relief area on the second drop.

If the player drops from knee height and the ball hits the ground and accidentally hits a person or object after hitting the ground and comes to rest in the relief area, that is a legal drop and you cannot elect to re-drop it and the player must play the ball as it lies in the relief area.

Determining the Drop Area. When you are allowed a drop, you can drop your ball *anywhere* in a "relief area" (but not nearer the hole). (Rule 14.3)

Even though a player may use a club shorter than the longest club in his bag (usually the driver) to measure, the relief area is defined under the new rule as an area as if the player used the length of the longest club in his bag (except the putter).

Remember the rule when you drop a ball, your ball must land in, come to rest and be played from the relief area. And, if it doesn't come to rest in the relief area, the player is to drop it again a second time, and if it again doesn't come to rest in the relief area, the player is to place the ball on the spot where the second ball hit the ground. But let's say the player places his ball on the spot where his second drop hit the ground and it still doesn't come to rest but rolls away. In that case, if a dropped ball fails to stay in the relief area after two drops, and then fails to remain on the spot when placed, it must be placed on the same spot again – before trying a different spot where it doesn't roll away. (14.3c (2))

Penalty Areas. A player can play his ball as it lies in a penalty area and ground his club, remove loose impediments, and take practice swings hitting the ground but if he decides not to, he must take penalty area relief. There are two types of penalty areas - red staked or lined and yellow staked or lined. (Rule 17).

Red Staked Penalty Area Relief. If the player decides to take red penalty relief, he takes 1 penalty stroke and has these 3 options for a red staked penalty area: 1) Go back to where he hit his shot into the penalty area and take a 1 club-length drop (i.e. take stroke and distance relief), or 2) Take back-on-the-line relief (i.e., go back as far as you like on an extension of a line from the hole to where the ball entered the penalty area) with a 1 club-length drop from the line no nearer the hole, or 3) Take a 2 club-length lateral drop from the point where the ball last crossed the edge of the penalty area no nearer the hole (Rule 17).

Yellow Staked Penalty Area Relief.   Except for taking a 2 club-length lateral drop from the point where the ball last crossed the edge of a red penalty area, the player has the same two options as he does for red staked penalty areas which are: 1) Go back to where the player hit his shot into the penalty area and take a 1 club-length drop (i.e. take stroke and distance relief), or 2) Take back-on-the-line relief (i.e., go back as far as you like on an extension of a line from the hole to where the ball entered the penalty area) with a 1 club-length drop from the line no nearer the hole (Rule 17).

Water Hazards Are Now Included in "Penalty Areas" The old rules referred to "water hazards" which might not have enabled you to take a lateral drop. Bodies of water are now referred to as penalty areas from which you can take lateral relief if it is a red staked penalty area. For yellow stakes, you can replay the shot or go back on the line from where your ball entered the yellow staked area. (Rule 17.1d). If it's not marked red or yellow, it's assumed to be red.

You Can Ground Your Club in a Penalty Area.
Under the old rule, if a player was in a hazard the
player received a general penalty if he touched the
ground with his body, or grounded your club, or
removed loose impediments.

Under the new rule, you can ground your club
behind the ball (even when your ball is in water),
remove loose impediments, or touch the ground. In
effect, you can play your ball out of a penalty just as
if you were playing the ball on the fairway or the
rough. (Rule 17)

Keep in mind, if you move your ball while removing
a loose impediment, you are penalized one-stroke
and you must replace your ball to its original
position before you moved it.

Keep in mind under new Rule 8.1a, you still can
incur a penalty for improving conditions for the
stroke so be careful when determining whether an
impediment is loose or not.

Opposite Side Relief for Penalty Areas. The
option to take relief on the opposite margin of a red
penalty area is still available by Local Rule. Under
the new rule, there is no longer an option for a

player to take relief on the opposite side of the penalty area. (Rule 17.1d)

No Requirement to Announce You Are Going to Lift Your Ball. Under the old rule, a player had to announce to the other player he was going to lift his ball to identify it.

Under the new rule, that is no longer required. This helps speed up play especially if the other player is across the fairway from you. Although you may want to announce it anyway to avoid confusion.

Before you lift your ball, first mark it and then lift it to identify it. You can only clean the ball to the extent necessary to identify it. You then replace the ball in the same place it came to rest.

Estimating Where to Replace Your Ball. If your ball is moved or lifted by someone else say for example another person lifts your ball by mistake, you can replace your ball on the same spot without penalty. If the exact spot is unknown, you estimate where your ball was to the best of your ability. (Rule 14.2c)

Keep in mind when the rules allow you to replace your ball, you must replace your ball on, under or against any fixed or growing things it had been at rest on.

And, if the spot of replacement is unknown then you use your best estimate in determining the spot to replace your ball.

Substituting a ball. Under the old rule there were conditions on when you could replace your ball.

Under the new rule, you can substitute another ball (or you are free to use your original ball) when taking free relief or penalty relief. (Rule 14.3)

3 Minute Search Time Limit for Lost Ball. Under the old rule, you were allowed 5 minutes to search for your ball.

Now the search time is reduced to 3 minutes. Check the time when you begin your searching. (Rule 18.2)

Moving Your Ball While Searching. Previously you were penalized one stroke if you moved your ball while searching for it. For example, if you accidentally step on your ball or nudge it while searching for it, you will have moved it.

Under the new rule, there is no one stroke penalty if you moved it accidentally while searching for your ball and you simply replace your ball if you (or others) accidentally move it when searching for it without penalty.

If you don't know the exact spot of the ball before it was moved, you can estimate the spot and replace your ball where you in good faith believe it was. This includes putting your ball back on, under or against anything it was on and as close to the spot as you best estimate in good faith. (Rule 7.4)

Lost Ball or OB. Under a new Local Rule, a golf course can elect to give players an option for dropping a ball without having to go back to the point where you hit the ball that became lost or went out of bounds and when they haven't played a provisional ball.

The golf course has the option to adopt a local rule allowing you to drop another ball and take a two-stroke penalty to speed up play. Check the local rules to see if the golf course has adopted this local rule.

The local rule helps a player who hasn't played a provisional ball from going back to the location of the previous stroke.

Under this local rule option, you drop your ball in a large relief area which is between two lines.

The first line is established using the "ball reference point" which is a line drawn from the hole to the ball reference point. The "ball reference point" is the point where the ball was lost or went out of bounds.

The second line is a line drawn from the hole to the "fairway reference point" and the fairway reference point is a point you mark on the nearest edge of the fairway no nearer the hole.

The relief area is between those two lines. Or in other words in the area between where the ball was lost or went out of bounds and the nearest edge of the fairway (no nearer the hole).

Also, this relief area is extended by two club lengths on the outside edges of the "ball reference point" and the "fairway reference point" (no nearer the hole).

This local rule is also not intended for professional play or high amateur competitions but intended to help speed up the pace of play.

The player is not allowed to use this option when his ball is known to be in a penalty area. If the player's ball is lost in a penalty area, the options for taking relief from a penalty area must be used instead.

The player is also not allowed to use this option when he has played a provisional ball.

The new rules refer to a Model Local Rule for a golf course to adopt which can be found here > USGA, Draft of Model Local Rule, see this link at bottom of page, "Stroke and Distance: Download the draft text as a PDF", and the link is >

http://www.usga.org/content/usga/home-page/rules-hub/rules-modernization/infographics/golf-s-new-rules--stroke-and-distance.html#expanded

Your Ball Accidentally Hits You or Your Equipment. Under the old rule, there was a general penalty incurred if your ball hits you or your equipment after you strike the ball.

Under the new rule there is no penalty if your ball strikes you, an opponent, or your equipment. However, this only applies if it happened accidentally. (Rule 11.1)

A general penalty is incurred if your ball should strike your foot or equipment if it was not an accident. For example, if you try to stop your ball with your foot or use one of your clubs or place a club in a position to stop your ball from going off the green, you would incur a general penalty (Rule 11.2a).

PACE OF PLAY

Play Promptly. Under the new rule, players are encouraged not to linger on the course or tees and to keep their pace of play consistent. Players are encouraged to not use more than 40 seconds once they become able to play their shot and there are no other distractions.

The penalty for unreasonably delaying play is revised to one penalty stroke for the first breach, a general penalty for the second breach, and disqualification for a third breach.

The new rules also encourage golf course committees to adopt a "Pace of Play" policy. Rule 5.6.

Ready Golf. There is a new rule which allows players to agree amongst themselves to allow other players who may be ready to take their shot to play before them to increase their group's pace of play. (Rule 6.4)

BUNKERS

Loose Impediments and Touching the Sand.
You are still penalized a stroke for testing the sand, grounding your club in front of or behind the ball, or touching the sand during a practice swing or your back swing.

Under the new rule, you can remove loose impediments. Also, there is no penalty if you happen to touch the sand accidentally or incidentally with a club but these accidental contacts with the sand have to be in locations other than grounding your club in front of or behind the ball or touching the sand during a practice swing or your back swing. You still cannot deliberately touch the sand to test it. (Rules 12.2a and 12.2b)

Declaring Your Ball Unplayable in a Bunker. The player has four options: (1) For one penalty stroke, the player may take stroke-and-distance relief and go back to the point where he last played the shot. (2) For one penalty stroke, the player may take back-on-the-line relief in the bunker. (3) For one penalty stroke, the player may take lateral relief in the bunker. (4) For a total of two penalty strokes, the player may take back-on-the-line relief outside the bunker based on a reference line going straight back from the hole through the spot of the original ball. (Rule 19.3)

Animal Holes.   Under the old rule, you were only given free relief from "burrowing animal" holes. The new rule allows you to take relief from all holes dug by animals irregardless if it was a burrowing animal or not. There is no free relief however from holes made by worms, insects and similar invertebrates. (Rule 16.1)

GREENS

Repairing Damage on the Green Without Penalty. A major change to repairing damage on the green is under Rule 13.1(c)2. You now can repair almost any damage, i.e., spike marks, pitch marks, etc. anywhere on the green.

Keep in mind you can repair only "damage" and you can't improve the line of your putt to the hole beyond repairing damage. That means you can't try to improve any natural imperfections (e.g., "aeration holes, natural surface imperfections or natural wear of the hole). (Rule 13.1b)

Wrong Green. Under the old rule, if your ball came to rest on the wrong green you had to pick it up and play your ball on the nearest point of relief off the green no closer to the hole. You could take your stance on the green itself to play your next shot.

Under the new rule, you are no longer allowed to take your stance on the green or to take a stance where the path of your swing might be over the surface of the green.

When you play your next shot, drop your ball so you won't be taking a stance on the green and so that it is not possible your swing path would contact the wrong green (Rule 13.1e).

You can touch the line of play on the putting green. Previously, you or your caddy were not allowed to touch the line of your putt without incurring a 1 stroke penalty. Under the new rule you or your caddy can touch the line of play of your putt on the green. (Rule 10.2b)

Accidentally Moving Your Ball on the Green. Previously if you accidentally moved your ball on the green you were penalized one stroke. Under the new rule, there is no penalty if you (or another player) accidentally move your ball on the green. (Rule 9.4; 9.5; 13.1c (1))

Your Ball Accidentally Moves as You Mark It or After You Replace It on the Green. Under new Rule 13.1d, if you mark your ball and your ball moves accidentally (e.g., your ball marker accidentally nudges your ball and moves it), or if you accidentally move your ball with your foot or club, you must replace it.

You only get to replace your ball if you have marked and lifted your ball. If your ball simply moves *before* you mark and lift your ball, you must play your ball from the spot it moves to.

If you replace your ball on the green and accidentally move it (e.g., by accidentally throwing your marker down or accidentally move the ball when you take your marker away), there is no penalty and you must replace your ball to its original position.

Under the new rule, if you replace your ball on the green and it moves by itself or for some unknown reason, you must replace it to its original position without penalty. (9.3; 13.1c (2) 1)

Hitting the Flagstick. There is no longer any penalty if you hit the flagstick with your putt. You have the option of leaving the flagstick in for a putt without incurring a penalty. (Rule 13.2a (2))

Ball Resting Against the Flagstick left in the hole. If a player's ball comes to rest against the flagstick left in the hole then if any part of the ball is in the hole below the surface of the putting green, the ball is treated as holed even if the entire ball is not below the surface.

This may be a grey area, but it seems if a ball is embedded in the side of the hole it is not holed unless the whole of the ball is below the surface, even if it is touching the flagstick. The words "resting against the flagstick" imply the ball is free to move so that it could fall into the hole if the flagstick wasn't there, but an embedded ball wouldn't, so the ball therefore needs to meet the definition of "holed out".

A Caddy Is Allowed to Mark and Clean a Ball on the Green. Previously caddies couldn't mark, lift and clean a ball without authorization. Under the new rules, caddies are allowed to mark and lift their player's ball from the green and clean it and either the player or the caddie can replace it. (Rule 14.1(b))

Lying a Club or Any Object on the Ground to Align a Shot. Previously, a player could lay a club down on the ground and use the shaft of the club to help align the shot or putt. Under the new rule that is no longer allowed anywhere on the course.

If you should lay a club down or any object on the ground to help your alignment and then take your stance, you would incur a general penalty.

You cannot avoid the general penalty by backing away and removing the club after taking your stance. (Rule 10.2b (3))

Caddies Can't Position Themselves to Assist a Shot or a Putt. Under the old rule, caddies could position themselves behind their player to help them line up a shot or putt.

This is no longer allowed. A caddy cannot stand behind you once you begin to take your stance for a shot or putt.

However, there is no penalty if the caddie should accidentally be standing behind you when he's not in the line of play and the caddie has no intention of giving any assistance to line up your shot. (Rule 10.2b (4))

Double Hitting the Ball. The old rule was if your club hit the ball twice in a single swing there was a one-stroke penalty. Under the new rule, there is no penalty and double or multiple hits in one stroke counts as only one stroke.

The player must play the next ball as it lies. (Rule 10.1a)

DAMAGED CLUBS

Use or Repair a Damaged Club. Under the new rule, a player can use a damaged club even if the player damaged the club in anger.

A player is also allowed to repair a damaged club and continue to use it. (Rule 4.1)

Replacing a Damaged Club. A player can only replace a damaged club if the damaged club occurred from an "outside influence" or "natural forces."

In other words, a player can replace a club if someone other than the player or his or her caddy damaged the club. (Rule 4.1)

Distance measuring devices are allowed. The new rule now is DMDs can be used on a golf course except where the golf course has a local rule prohibiting the use of DMDs.

Most every golf course allows DMDs but check the local rules to make sure there is no rule against DMDs before you use one. (Rule 4.3)

Maximum Score. To help pace of play, there is a new stroke play format called "Maximum Score."

The new rules allow a golf course to use a Maximum Score format and have players pick up on a hole once the player reaches the maximum score for that hole.

For example, the Committee can set the maximum at double bogey (or any maximum score they decide) for each hole. The new rule provides under "maximum score" a player is not disqualified once the player reaches the maximum score and picks up for that hole.

CODE OF CONDUCT VIOLATIONS

Getting overly angry, or any outrageous conduct may violate the golf course's code of conduct.

Under the new rule, a golf course can adopt a code of conduct and disqualify a player for not acting in accordance with the course's code of conduct during play. (Rules 1.2a and 1.2b)

We'd love to hear from you!

Image from Creative Commons

"There usually is a way to do things better and there is opportunity when you find it."

- Thomas Edison

If you have a different opinion on the rules of golf, please let us know and email us your thoughts at TeamGolfwell@gmail.com. We love to hear from our readers, and we answer every email.

Thank you very much for your interest in our book and we hope you enjoyed our book and it helps you settle rule issues.

If you liked our book, we would appreciate your leaving a very brief review on Amazon or Goodreads. Thank you very much. Happy Golfing!

Sincerely,

The TeamGolfwell

www.TeamGolfwell.com

GOLFWELL

www.TeamGolfwell.com

About the Author

TeamGolfwell are bestselling authors. Their books have sold thousands of copies including several #1 bestsellers in golf and sports humor.

Contact us at TeamGolfwell@Gmail.com for anything. We love to hear from our fans!

www.TeamGolfwell.com

Team Golfwell's Other Books

WALK THE WINNING WAYS OF GOLF'S GREATESTS
GOLFING GREATS' ADVICE TO YOUNG GOLFERS

Walk the Winning Ways of Golf's Greatests

For Young Golfers, Junior Golfers, First Tee

"Golf's New Rules" by TeamGolfwell

Team Golfwell's Other Books

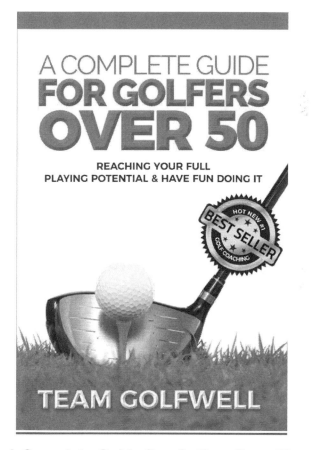

A Complete Guide For Golfers Over 50: Reaching Your Full Playing Potential & Have Fun Doing It. (Over 300 pages)

[1] USGA, http://www.usga.org/content/usga/home-page/rules-hub/rules-modernization/major-changes/relief-for-an-embedded-ball.html

[2] USGA, http://www.usga.org/content/usga/home-page/rules-hub/rules-modernization/major-changes/taking-relief.html

[3] USGA, http://www.usga.org/content/usga/home-page/rules-hub/rules-modernization/major-changes/new-procedure-for-dropping-a-ball.html

[4] USGA, http://www.usga.org/content/usga/home-page/rules-hub/rules-modernization/major-changes/areas-the-committee-may-mark-as-penalty-areas.html

[5] USGA, http://www.usga.org/content/usga/home-page/rules-hub/rules-modernization/major-changes/substitution-of-a-ball-always-allowed-when-taking-relief.html

[6] USGA, http://www.usga.org/content/usga/home-page/rules-hub/rules-modernization/major-changes/reduced-time-for-search-before-a-ball-is-lost.html

[7] USGA, http://www.usga.org/content/usga/home-page/rules-hub/rules-modernization/major-changes/ball-moved-during-search.html

[8] USGA, http://www.usga.org/content/usga/home-page/rules-hub/rules-modernization/major-changes/golfs-new-rules-stroke-and-distance.html

[9] USGA, http://www.usga.org/content/usga/home-page/rules-hub/rules-modernization/major-changes/ball-in-motion-accidentally-deflected.html

[10] USGA, http://www.usga.org/content/usga/home-page/rules-hub/rules-modernization/major-changes/encouraging-prompt-pace-of-play.html

[11] Ibid.

[12] USGA, http://www.usga.org/content/usga/home-page/rules-hub/rules-modernization/major-changes/moving-or-touching-loose-impediments-or-sand-in-a-bunker.html

[13] USGA, http://www.usga.org/content/usga/home-page/rules-hub/rules-modernization/major-changes/unplayable-ball-in-a-bunker.html

[14] USGA, http://www.usga.org/content/usga/home-page/rules-hub/rules-modernization/major-changes/repairing-damage-on-the-putting-green.html

[15] USGA, http://www.usga.org/content/usga/home-page/rules-hub/rules-modernization/major-changes/touching-the-line-of-play-on-a-putting-green.html

[16] USGA, http://www.usga.org/content/usga/home-page/rules-hub/rules-modernization/major-changes/no-penalty-for-moving-a-ball-on-the-putting-green.html

[17] USGA, http://www.usga.org/content/usga/home-page/rules-hub/rules-modernization/major-changes/ball-played-from-the-putting-green-hits-unattended-flagstick-in-hole.html

[18] USGA, http://www.usga.org/content/usga/home-page/rules-hub/rules-modernization/major-changes/ball-accidentally-struck-more-than-once.html

[19] USGA, http://www.usga.org/content/usga/home-page/rules-hub/rules-modernization/major-changes/use-of-clubs-damaged-during-round.html

[20] USGA, http://www.usga.org/content/usga/home-page/rules-hub/rules-modernization/major-changes/adding-clubs-to-replace-a-club-damaged-during-round.html

[21] USGA, http://www.usga.org/content/usga/home-page/rules-hub/rules-modernization/major-changes/use-of-distance-measuring-devices.html

[22] USGA, http://www.usga.org/content/usga/home-page/rules-hub/rules-modernization/major-changes/maximum-score--form-of-stroke-play.html

[23] USGA, http://www.usga.org/content/usga/home-page/rules-hub/rules-modernization/major-changes/code-of-player-conduct.html

Printed in Great Britain
by Amazon

85399974R00025